SELLING 1,000,000+

Per Year
IN HVAC HOME COMFORT
&
INDOOR AIR QUALITY
(IAQ)

SELLING 1,000,000+

Per Year
IN HVAC HOME COMFORT
&
INDOOR AIR QUALITY
(IAQ)

◆

Or anything else you want to sell. The principles do not change only the product.

Michael Youngs

—*Winner Comfortech IDOL 2004*

—*Certified Indoor Environmentalist*

—*1,000,000+ Residential Replacement Specialist*

—*Published HVAC Industry Writer*

iUniverse, Inc.

New York Lincoln Shanghai

SELLING 1,000,000+

Per Year

IN HVAC HOME COMFORT

&

INDOOR AIR QUALITY

(IAQ)

Or anything else you want to sell. The principles do not change only the product.

iUniverse books may be ordered through booksellers or by contacting:

iUniverse
2021 Pine Lake Road, Suite 100
Lincoln, NE 68512
www.iuniverse.com
1-800-Authors (1-800-288-4677)

ISBN: 0-595-34960-9

Printed in the United States of America

Contents

Acknowledgements

This book is dedicated to all the people who believed in me, and gave me a chance.

Special dedication and love go out to my wife Karen and my two wonderful boys Ryan and Nathan. You three give me the power and enthusiasm to make my dreams come true. Also to my wonderful mother and father who have never doubted me and gave me the love and support to grow into the person I am today, thanks!

I also give special dedication to Mark & Sue Meacham, two of the most wonderful people and employers on the face of the earth. Without both of you, I would not have had the opportunity to do what I am doing today, and would not have been able to achieve what I am achieving today. Thanks for believing in me and giving me that chance in 2002! Mark E. Meacham, Inc. is truly a special place.

Many thanks also go out to my friend and colleague Charlie Greer who has inspired me to be the best of the best within the HVAC/R industry.

Thanks to all, and best wishes!

May happiness abound each and every one of you forever and ever.

I hope and pray that all who read this book find the inspiration inside them to achieve whatever it is you would like to achieve.

BELIEVE IT AND YOU CAN ACHIEVE IT!

Michael Youngs can be reached by emailing:
mjyoungs@charter.net

YOU **CAN** CLIMB ANY MOUNTAIN!
SET YOUR COURSE AND DO IT!
BELIEVE IN YOURSELF...

1

Sales 101

Before we start talking about sales techniques and what it takes to be a great salesperson, let's first talk about what it really takes to do anything well.

As in everything else in life you need to have a **positive attitude**. Whatever it may be that you set out to do if your attitude is poor your results will be poor as well. Something about a greater power that I can't explain stands behind everything we do and the results we achieve. If you believe you can do it, your right, and if you believe you can't do it, you are probably right as well.

If you have the attitude that nothing works, and everything you try goes wrong, than I suggest you send this book back to me for a full refund. If your attitude is that you are looking for a quick way to be a great salesperson and make a lot of money without hard work, forget it! I'm not saying that you have to spend every waking hour in sales related functions I just mean that you need to do what it takes to be successful. Being successful has a different meaning for everyone. So whatever success means to you, think positive, and YES you can do it.

I find that most successful people have a great balance in life. They have spent time and energy in the following areas:

- Personal
- Professional
- Financial
- Physical
- Spiritual

If you work on all of those areas, in whatever order you choose, ultimately the happiness and success you are seeking is near. In no way will I speak about any religion or spiritual values, as this is within you and means many different things to people. I am just sharing that many successful people have worked hard in the areas I have outlined above. I can tell you from direct experience that if any of those areas are far out of whack than total happiness and contentment will not be possible.

We will talk more about these areas and how to concentrate on a plan to evaluate where you may be at in any of those areas. We will also look at ways to plan, track and evaluate where you need to go and what you need to do in order to achieve whatever it is you are hoping to achieve. For some people it may mean financial independence, and for others it may mean a feeling of well-being, a feeling of being accepted. It may also mean for some that they have someone to enjoy life with, and a true purpose and direction in life. Whatever your stumbling block may be, we will take a look at how to overcome these obstacles and get the movement and strength of positive energy and positive momentum.

Chances are that once you get moving in that direction, and make up your mind to make it happen, no one and no circumstance will be able to stop you.

You are in charge of your life and your destiny. Take control and be the person you want to be. Do what it is you want to do. No one else is going to do it for you, they are working on themselves. Don't just stand there, take action today. Today is the first day of the rest of your life, hold on and enjoy the ride.

For me, learning is an important part of my development and success. I have found great power and knowledge from many people in my life. The first inspiration I ever had as it relates to sales was from Mr. Zig Ziglar. In my opinion he is by far the best of the best at sales and sales motivation. You will find that much of my positive attitude thoughts and processes are derived from the teachings of the master. Think about it, "a check up from the neck up". That sounds like the silliest thing you have ever heard, but it is for real. Your head needs to be clear and your thought process has to be precise. If you don't have a clear cut plan, and a way to execute that plan, than the results will be in direct proportion to poor planning. Poor results are a direct result of poor planning. Look at professional sports teams. Do they have a plan? Do they work on that plan? Do they get results that are proportionate to the plan?

Many of you are saying to yourself, "yeah but I'm not that good", "they or him or her is better than me". Stop that type of thinking immediately! If you think that way the chances are that is exactly the result you are going to get. Positive attitude along with positive thoughts produce positive results. Believe me, and the millions of others that have experienced this phenomenon.

Being happy and successful at whatever you do doesn't happen overnight. It is a combination of many events that you put together to compile the success factor. Believe me, I made my share of mistakes and have been down the wrong road more than once. Finally at age thirty-nine I truly understand what it takes to make your life whatever you decide to make it. Life and its experiences are not about good or bad luck, it's about what you do with the opportunities placed in front of you. Like the old saying says: "When life deals you lemons, make lemonade". How true that statement is, and always will be.

The outcome of any situation depends upon how and what you do with that situation. If you choose to learn from each and every challenge in a positive manner it will make you better and stronger. If you choose to let life's challenges put you down, it will take twice as long to get the momentum back to the same place you started. Keep the balls of positive momentum going and it is impossible to stop. Many people along the way will certainly give you advice. Some may actually be helpful and some advice may be out of envy or jealousy, choose and use this advice carefully. Remember, no one pays the price for your actions and decisions more than you and your loved ones.

Now that we have the first step clear we can begin to move on. If you still don't get that you must have positive attitude, than please turn back and start over at page one. If you know you can do it, and feel it inside that your success and happiness are right there, then move on to the following pages and have fun. Your life will never, ever be the same!!

2

Now what

◆

THE MINDSET

"IT'S NOT AN ALARM CLOCK, IT'S AN OPPORTUNITY CLOCK."

Now that you have moved on to this section that means you have what it takes. PMA! (Positive Mental Attitude). If you ask all in my path throughout my career and life, they will all share my unwavering enthusiasm and my positive attitude. Even during the toughest challenges and events in my life, my attitude remained upbeat and positive, even when it was very hard to do. And believe me the challenges were many.

Enough about that. Now you must decide if you are truly doing what you like to do. Do you enjoy going to your office or place of business or do you dread Mondays? Are you happiest on Fridays and Holidays when you don't have to work? It is very important to like what you do, because to get excited and have enthusiasm for something you don't enjoy is very hard. If you hate your office, your co-workers, your boss and the industry you are in, please put this book down and open up the newspaper and find a job you can enjoy. I can teach you all the things in the world to help you become a great marketing person, a great closer, a great phone professional, but if you're not in the right industry and place, none of my insight will help. If you are in the right industry, in the right place, then move on it's time.

It is now time for you to decide what is important to you. Is it a financial goal? Do you want a new house? Do you want a new car? Is it a certain position you would like? Whatever it is, stop now and go someplace where it is quiet. When you arrive at that place take two minutes to just breathe. Now, concentrate on how it will feel when you reach that place…What does the house look like? How does that car drive? How is the new office with that new position? How excited and upbeat does this achievement make you feel? How do your friends and family feel about this achievement? Spend three un-interrupted minutes with your eyes closed imagining this place, thing or feeling. Now, do this everyday until that comes true than make another one and do the same thing. Try it, what have you got to lose?

Now it is time to figure out exactly how and what path you can take to get there. You need to place a value on the item if it is materialistic. If the item does not carry a dollar value, then you must place the ultimate goal in writing on a piece of paper. This piece of paper must be kept with you at all times. This is between you and maybe the closest person or people to you. If anyone may not feel as positive about you achieving this goal, and may cast any negativism on this goal, than do not share it with anyone. Once you get to that point the GRAND FIRE will happen where you burn the paper and move on to the next written goal. This is a very important step. In fact, if you can write that several times on that piece of paper it will further ingrain this goal in your sub-conscience. It also helps to make statements on that piece of paper like: "My new car is so nice". "I feel great in this new car". "I am so happy I sold 1 million dollars this year". You get the point. Make the goal, write it down, believe in your goal, and now you are in motion to start moving towards this goal.

3

The goal

"A written, realistic, prioritized, measurable achievement, which will be the result of the specific effort."

Now that you have established your goal, whatever it may be, we have to plan the actions necessary to make that goal or dream a reality. I find that many in the sales profession are number or dollar motivated. Some may be percentage motivated, such as closing ratio, or market growth, or percent over objective. But in some form or fashion to be a motivated, success driven sales professional, close attention to numbers is part of your job description.

Throughout my career I have worked with, worked for, and trained many sales professionals. Some good, some great and some not so good. Sales is not an easy profession by any means, although it is the highest paid easiest work. In no other job can you earn in a minute, a day, or an hour what you can earn as a successful salesperson. Most high energy, high production salespeople I have met are motivated by dollars. The opportunity to earn big money, and the benefits that come along with those earnings. The benefits for their families and themselves. Let's face it; we all take personal pride in being a good provider. (Or at least we should).

Because most sales professionals are motivated at least in part, by money, my example will demonstrate the process of setting a goal to reach that objective.

Let's say you want to make $100,000.00 this year.
Your commission is 10% of every sale.
Therefore you need to sell $1,000,000.00 worth of product. ($1,000,000 x 10%)
That means you need to sell approximately $83,334.00 per month.

<u>Break it down further:</u>

You need to sell $19,380.00 per week. ($83,334.00 divided by 4.3 weeks per month)

If you work 5 days per week you need to concentrate on $3,876.00 per day.

If you work 8 hours per day you need to sell $484.50 per hour.

Now, you need to take into account personal days, holidays, vacations and time off.

I call this breaking it down to the ridiculous. Once you understand and practice this for yourself, you can also use this technique to soften the investment figure for your client. The investment is not $14,800.00 it is only about $13.70 per day. (I used $14,800.00 divided by 36 months, then divide by 30 days per month). Compared to the amount you save in fuel with the high efficiency equipment you are actually making money.

In order to reach whatever goal you are going to reach you have to understand how it breaks down. You can't "hope" for the best. You have to understand how the numbers work, and what its going to take to get there. Wouldn't you agree that when you break them down they seem more achievable? (We will get into closing questions, and assumptive statements later). When you start using closing statements and assumptive statements without realizing it, you are on your way! Doesn't it sound easy? Wouldn't you agree this works? Don't you like the way it sounds? It's an easy way to break it down, isn't it? (Get what I mean?) That's not nice; I could go on for pages asking assumptive questions. (A favorite of my friend Charlie Greer). Practice this daily at work and at home. It will become second nature, and you will never be stumped again.

Now that you understand how to break down your goal in terms of dollars, you need to understand how many customers you need to see. You need to understand, track and evaluate your closing ratio. You need to also understand your average sale amount.

You need to make the goal attainable and if you find your not getting close, you need to re-evaluate your goal and start from the beginning. A goal is only good if it is reachable and realistic. Setting goals that you cannot reach is truly setting yourself up for failure and disappointment, and you will have nobody to blame but yourself.

<u>Understanding your closing ratio and qualified appointment needs:</u>

Let's say your closing ratio is 40%

Your average sale is $5,200.00

That means your commission is $520.00 per sale @ 10%

Remember you need to make about $1,938.00 per week

That means you need to close about 3.72 people per week (Round up to 4 per week).

(I like to round up). This accounts for vacations and cancellations, if you have any.

If you close 40% you will have to present to 10 people per week. (10 x 40% = 4 sales)

Breaking it down you need about 2 appointments per day.

If your company is not providing an average of 2 appointments per day, then you need to work your referrals, cold calling and home shows better.

Breaking down your dollars needed and understanding how many appointments you need to reach that goal makes it easier. Actually it makes it possible. Without this complete understanding, there is no way, except by complete luck, that you will ever meet your goals. Contact me at mjyoungs@charter.net and I will assist you in setting up your goal based tracking.

Once you have a thorough understanding of where your mindset must be, what your goal is and how you get there, the rest is practice. Practice makes perfect. You have to be prepared for every move. Sales is like chess, except you don't have the time to make your move, it needs to be instantaneous and has to be sincere.

One of the biggest problems I have found while training or working with sales-people is they do not listen properly. Or maybe they listen but they do not hear. The customer will tell you everything you need to know, if you will listen. Most salespeople are formulating an answer while the customer is talking. How can you formulate an answer when you haven't even heard the questions yet? Then you wonder why your response to their question didn't close the sale. The answer is, you really didn't understand the question because you were not fully listening. Listen and take notes! Ask and listen.

4

The process

"A systematic series of actions directed to some end."

Many of you who have read the article about me in Contracting Business (February 2005) written by Charlie Greer, are already aware of my process. If you are reading this book, that tells me that you either didn't understand the article written by Charlie, or you didn't practice what was said. Therefore, we are going to go through it again. This process is not something you can read once and be a master of. You need to fully understand the psychology behind why each step is important. If you miss just one part of the process you might as well not do any of it. Believe me, I have tried to take short cuts and not do certain things. The only thing that happens is that my closing ratio goes down, and my customer doesn't get to enjoy the awesome system I could have installed. The company and my family don't get to enjoy the income that I lost out on by not following the process. Missing steps creates nothing good.

Prior to going on any appointment the process needs to be clearly defined and written within your organization. This needs to be done by you and the management or owners of the business. This process needs to become company policy and fully understood by anyone and everyone involved. A deliberate breach of this policy is grounds for corrective action or termination as stated in the policies and procedures. The importance of the process has to be enforced. Call it a special name, such as: XYZ Corp. Business Development Plan. Get the people who are involved with the process involved with the development. People are more likely to follow the process if they take ownership of the plan. They are more likely to take ownership if they have a hand in developing it. Each and every step is important, and every person in the process is just as important as the next.

This development program starts from the minute the phone rings. Each person needs to be crossed trained in answering the phone. Anyone from the controller to the owner to the groundskeeper needs to be trained to take that call with a smile. If the employee has any possibility of answering the phone, they need to be trained and on the same page as the next person. The only way to make this process uniform is by training and developing phone scripts for the call taker to follow. Each phone script needs to clearly define the questions and what action to take with the call. The single most important thing is capturing the persons name and address along with telephone number if appropriate. With today's telemarketing awareness, some rapport should be made prior to asking for that number. Nothing drives me crazier than a customer service person saying, "They just needed their refrigerator fixed". That customer service representative just let a potential customer or relationship off the phone. Isn't it possible that the person on the other end of the phone might have heat or air-conditioning? Isn't it possible that at some point now or in the future that person may have a need for a HVAC/R system or service? What would be wrong with saying, "Great, thanks for calling, I would be happy to assist you, could you please give me your name? O.K. Peggy, would you mind giving me your address? This needs to be done before we tell them we don't fix refrigerators. Then immediately a thank you introduction packet needs to be sent to that customer explaining your company and their services.

Believe me, that when the need for your services does arrive, the likelihood they call you now is 100% better than if we didn't offer any help at all. Maybe the refrigeration they were talking about was for their father's fifteen grocery stores. Maybe the refrigeration they were looking to get repaired was for their restaurant. If we don't ask questions and take the time to do a bit of probing we will never know.

Nobody knows how much business we all have lost by not asking the right questions. Or by not taking a second to show you do care. Maybe you were in a hurry and had your friend waiting on the other line so you were happy the call didn't take that long. There really is no great way at measuring how many lost opportunities happen in the first call. There is some telephone software and tracking that let's us know how many calls we receive, and then we can track where each call went and decide if appropriate action is being taken. This is expensive and time consuming, and frankly, if we have to track and monitor the people answering our phones to that extent, than maybe we have the wrong people answering the phone.

Did you ever notice that when you call a car dealership to ask about a car you had seen in the paper or on the car lot, the salesperson says, "I am back in the service department, if you give me your name and number I will get back to you with that information." Now most people do not call a car dealership often enough to catch on, but guess what they are doing? Capturing your information! Call taking 101. Now I am not going to give up all the auto dealerships secrets, but I may share a few throughout the book. Only the ones that contain honesty and integrity will I ever use in my process today. In fact, the training professionals in the auto business do ghost calling and ghost shopping to monitor if in fact these techniques are being utilized. In fact, when they call the dealership they often record the call to share with the owner or general manager as a form of training and monitoring. Now do you wonder why the turnover in that business is so extremely high?

I am not going to give you all the written scripts for this process, but certainly if you are interested, you can contact me and I will help you develop those scripts. In fact you can also get the book written by the late great Tom McCart and that will help you as well. Tom McCart was one of the greatest sales pioneers in our industry, and developed the "No Secrets Training System." Inside that training manual you will find scripts and actual usable forms for completing most of what we will talk about in this book. I had never had the honor of meeting the man, but have watched the video named From the Sky Up, the story of Tom McCart. I will tell you that interview with Charlie Greer is touching and I urge you to watch it as well. Please feel free to contact me directly if you wish to obtain a copy of that publication or video. You can also get one on-line @ www. hvacprofitboosters.com

After your business development plan is structured and everyone understands how calls are to be handled you are on your way. You thought we were going to go right into the techniques and the process, your wrong, first things first. Now we are ready to talk about the actual home comfort recommendation process. Let's go!

5

The pre-appointment preparation

I like to call this the pre-appointment. Normally at the end of the day I take a look at my next day's schedule. I have a schedule in the company TMS program, and the lead folders are marked in the corresponding day. I have five separate folders, Monday through Saturday, and each day's appointments are placed in the corresponding day's folder.

When I take out the next day's folder's I pay attention to the time of my first appointment, the location of that appointment and each appointment after. I then run a map quest from the office to the first appointment, and then from that appointment to the next. I then pay close attention to where the lead came from. I want to see if it is from service, and if it is I will take a look at the service file and pay attention to the technician's notes. What type of equipment do they have? Is it oil or gas? Do they have a furnace or boiler? Was the customer a referral? If so, from whom? If it is a referral I will take a look at the file of the person they were referred from, and take note of the type of equipment they bought, how much they paid, and who was the comfort specialist.

During my search of the next day's activities I am going to gather any customer letters or comment cards from any clients we may have that live in their neighborhood. If not in their neighborhood, then in their town. I am going to make copies of these and enter them in my book. I call the book "why buy here book". I call it that to myself, and not to my clients. This book has many items in it which we will discuss at greater length later.

All of this is prior to ever heading to the appointment. I will also notice anything that doesn't sound correct, and if necessary call the customer to probe a little prior to the appointment. The more leg work you do up-front, the better the appointment will go. If you do happen to make that call, please start it out as a friendly appointment confirmation. I will say something like, "hi is this Bob? Hi

Bob, this is Michael Youngs from Mark E. Meacham; did I catch you at a bad time? No, that's great, I was just looking at tomorrows schedule and noticed that we are scheduled to meet at your house at 6:00pm, is that correct? Do you mind if I ask you a couple of questions so that I make sure I bring the right literature with me tomorrow? No o.k. it says you are looking for a price on a new furnace, is that right? Good Bob, well you have called the right place. What makes you **feel** that you need a new furnace? How did you hear about us Bob? Alright, that sounds good Bob I'll see you tomorrow at 6:00pm. If you have any questions before that please feel free to call me on my cell phone @ _____ ".

This conversation should not be about selling yourself or the company; it is only about confirming the appointment. If you happen to get some more information that's great, if not, no big deal. You have just shown more professionalism than 90% of your competitors. Also, when people get to speak to you a bit prior to the appointment you are already on better ground than most that speak for the first time at the home. Whatever you do, do not speak about pricing. If it comes up in the phone conversation simply answer by saying, "Bob, we will go over all of that tomorrow evening". And move on.

6

Appointment time

Make sue you have your driving directions to your appointment. I like to run those the prior day if possible. If you are going from one appointment to another make sure you run the directions from the first appointment to your next appointment to assure your timeliness. Make sure you take the time of day and traffic into consideration, and always leave yourself plenty of time in case of an accident or an unplanned delay. If for any reason at all you are running behind, make sure you call your customer as early as possible to inform them that you are running late. Your timeliness and consideration of their schedule is a great tribute to your professionalism. These pre-steps to the appointment are very important as they lay the ground work for the "first impression". Remember you only get one chance to make a first impression.

Prior to your arrival make sure your appearance is professional and that you are shaven, your shirt is clean and your breath is tolerable. A little forethought in this arena goes a long way in the unconscious impression left in your customers mind. I am a firm believer in logo shirts that match the logo on the truck along with a logo identification clearly defining who you are, your position and who you work for.

Your pre-arrival tour of the neighborhood is very important. Arrive to the neighborhood 10-15 minutes prior to your scheduled appointment time. I call this the pre-sale neighborhood inspection. When you take this tour you want to pay attention to the average home age, the landscaping, window units and any competitors working in the area. This information will give you a good idea of what's going on their. Do not pre-judge your client based upon your observations. This alone is a major problem with many sales professionals. If you go into the appointment thinking your customer does not have the financial means to buy, you are setting yourself up for failure. You have no idea. Maybe a rich uncle just died, maybe the house was left to them, and maybe they just refinanced and took a huge amount of money out. YOU just don't know. This tour is a simple investigation to learn more about your potential client.

A very important part of this tour is paying attention to the air-conditioning units in the homes. Are all the outdoor condensing units a certain brand, and you offer or prefer a different brand? Is that brand most likely installed by a competitor you are familiar with? You need to know who is working in your market, what they are selling and how they are selling. As a sales professional you need to be fully aware of this information. Never ever say anything bad about your competitor. Do not talk badly about any specific brand or product and never say anything bad about the sales person or Competitor Company. You need to however, work into your presentation everything that your company does that you know they do not do. Let the customer come to their own conclusion about what's right or wrong, and what is best for them. Sell value! The Armed Forces always has intelligence about their enemy, and you should be the same way. I'm not saying invite your competitor over to a friends for a free estimate, but if you're good you will! Find out how they sell and what they sell and why. Be prepared, your going to be the best. The plan is what sets you apart. The determination is what gets you there.

7

The initial approach

"Sounds like we are flying a plane"
"We are, the flight is your life"

Arrive in front of the house about five minutes prior to the scheduled appointment time. Make sure you park in front of the house, and make sure they can see your clean well lettered truck when they open the door. Never park in the driveway, unless it is a very long driveway. Nothing worse than having to move your truck in the middle of a presentation because your blocking little Bobby's car. This could be potentially sale threatening and ruin your positive sale momentum. You may also leak oil on the driveway and leave a long-lasting negative impression.

Have your folder ready prior to arrival. You do not want to seem disorganized upon your arrival. It is likely they are watching you as you pull up. Believe me they want to see what you're driving and what you look like as badly as you want to see them.

Walk diligently up to the front door and knock three times. (Isn't that a song?). Make sure not to knock too loud, but make sure they know you are there. After knocking step back away from the door. I do this so that they do not feel intimidated when they open the door. This way they can also see over me and see my truck directly behind me. Subliminally they are matching my truck with the logo on my shirt. From a very young age the "uniform" presents professionalism in our lives. When they are opening the door I will often extend my company badge toward them a bit to give them the safe and secure feeling we all want and enjoy. I will then say, "Hi, I'm Mike from Mark E. Meacham".

Once you are invited into their home you want to enter just inside the front door so that the door may be closed. At that point I will offer a hand shake to all parties in the front entry. I will give a pat or two to scruffy the dog as well. If their dog likes you, there is a good chance they will like you to. Not a bad idea to have a Scooby snack for scruffy, but make sure you ask permission first. Nothing worse for a sale than having scruffy go into a seizure because of an allergic reaction. Even I would have a hard time closing that sale. (Well, maybe not. I would probably take time to talk a lot about indoor air quality and the allergic reactions caused by indoor particulate matter, or give Scruffy CPR).

Now you have made it into the front entry way of the home. It is time to put on your Dr. HVAC booties. Yes, shoe covers! I know you are saying, "Do people really use those?" Yes, people really use those! Many times the customer will say out of courtesy, "don't bother", or, "you don't need to put those on". My reply is this, "I'm sorry Bill; it is our policy to always wear these in your home. If I didn't wear these I would feel like I am cheating you and the Company and I would never do either of those". This is a great way to set the stage of professionalism. This is also about the third thing you have done that your competitors probably haven't done. You are just building a case step by step. All these little things lead to one big thing. Higher closing ratios with higher average sales along with happier customers. Happy customers send more referrals and then it starts all over again. You sell more, you earn more, and live happily ever after.

8

You're in the front door,
now what?

Once the initial approach into the castle is complete it is time to work on several key areas. In most cases you should be on a first name basis with your customer. I love to play a game I call "the name game". I try and see how many times I can incorporate their names into our regular conversation. The way that works is like this, "thanks, Bill, would you show me where the thermostats are located"? Great Bill, do you normally keep it set at one temperature, or....? "Bill and Janet, would you mind if I asked you a few questions to see what you are hoping to accomplish, and how I may be able to assist you?" "At that point we can start to determine what you may need if anything"?

The idea is to make this conversational. This is not a grilling of your customer. Many salespeople are too rigid in their analysis or initial approach. If you make your customer uncomfortable at this point it is twice as hard to turn them around and ultimately close the deal. Asking questions is important, but listening is more important, I mean truly listening and hearing what they are saying. Whether they realize it or not, every word out of their mouth is another step or "clue" to the end result which is earning their business. If you truly don't understand their needs and hot buttons you will not be able to involve them emotionally, and if you don't involve them emotionally your closing ratio will be low.

The structured needs analysis is a guideline of what questions you need to ask. You will not have to or be required to ask every question on every call. This is where you need to use your smarts and decide what is appropriate to ask in order to completely understand your customers buying motives. What is important to them? Is it efficiency? Is it indoor air-quality? Is it even temperatures? Is it ultra quiet operation? Is it utility savings or understanding how the new high-efficiency system actually pays for itself? You need to know these things in order to make the recommendations that fit what their true needs are. Their needs may be real or imaginary but they are the emotional trigger that causes them to go forward with you, your company and your equipment.

Please contact me so that we may discuss how to format your "needs analysis" for you, your customer, your company and your market. You can start by right now writing down the top twenty reasons you think your customers decide to go with you or someone else. We can than format those into "soft" questions that obtain the answer you are looking to obtain. I truly love questions regarding indoor air-quality. Questions like, "does anyone in your home suffer from asthma or aller-gies" "Does anyone in the house seem to get a lot of colds during the year? "When one person in the home gets sick does it seem that everyone gets sick? "Have you ever noticed that anyone in the household suffers from dry skin? "How about itchy or watery eyes" You get the idea by now, I hope!

You are only asking questions and writing down their answers. You are not mak-ing any suggestions or additional comments at this point. Your only response will be to further investigate the answer that was given. You are going levels deeper in the pain they feel or experience as a result of this condition/problem/comfort concern.

If they say, "Jenny has terrible allergies in the spring" your response is, "really…does she see an allergist for this condition?" "Is she required to take any medication as a result of this problem"? The answer to the question really is not that important, it is the fact that you are asking the question and are going to assist in this problem during your comfort recommendations.

After completion of the needs analysis and after some idle talk just getting to know each other it is almost time to move on. Prior to moving on you must pro-vide a re-cap of what you were told. This is very important because it can be used several times later in your presentation and during pre and post close. The re-cap goes like this, "o.k. Bill and Janet, thanks for that information, this will help me determine any recommendations to make in regards to your health, safety and home comfort". Look at the key words in that phrase: Bill, Janet, thanks, infor-mation, help, recommendations, health, safety, home comfort. The next step is phrased in this manner, "so what you told me was that Jenny suffers from aller-gies", "your master bedroom is too cold, your den is too hot", "and you can't stand your hard earned money going to the utility company". "Is that informa-tion correct"? "Is there anything I left out or anything you would like to add"?

You asked the questions, now make sure you listen. Take notes even if it's just brief words. You are differentiating, building credibility and showing that you care about their needs.

This process should be done sitting down wherever the customer is comfortable. Normally when you ask them about some initial questions they will take you to the conversation place in their house. I like to go into the sun room, the three season porch or the family room. This is where they have conversations, and that is exactly what we are doing, having a conversation. The final recommendations cannot be done in this same place. The final recommendations need to be done where they conduct business. Many times this will be where they pay bills, such as an office area or the dining room table. Believe me after you take the step by step approach they will be ready to go to the decision place wherever that may be for them. Do not conduct business standing in the cellar or the attic, and especially not in the front entry way, as this is only feet from the front door. Subconsciously people are not comfortable in making large buying decisions at the front door. Within a years time they may buy some Girl Scout cookies or a subscription to a magazine, but they are not accustomed to spending thousands at the front door.

If at the beginning you establish the process and take control with an up-front contract it will make this process easier. The up-front contract is not as rigid as it sounds, it is simply a verbal understanding of how things will happen, and the process set-forth. We will do this, that, and this and then I may be able to make recommendations at that point. "Does that sound fair Bill and Janet"? That's all. It is a verbal agreement to the steps that will be taken in order to close a sale. This also gets them making decisions up-front, or at least answering pointed questions. No surprises, everything is up-front and explained. If something is not understood or seems to be unclear you go back, re-trace your steps, clarifying and keep moving forward.

9

Measurement with customer
involvement

This is a great point to really get your customer involved. You ask them to take you room by room so that you can measure the house to ensure proper sizing and air-flow. During this process you are able to see many, many things. "O.K. Bill and Janet, now we need to measure the house room by room, can you take me on the tour? Now you are giving them some control. (But only briefly) You can determine a boat load about your customer during this three hour tour. Not really three hours, that's just a figment of speech taken from Gilligan's Island.

While you are going through the house you can observe their buying habits and their living habits. Does the kitchen have top-of-the-line appliances? Do they buy the best? Or do they have the least expensive value type items? Are their humidifiers? De-humidifiers? Air-filtration devices? Window units? Pay attention to all of these things as these items tell you allot about your customer.

One of the biggest reasons to measure the house room by room is to have your customer involved with you. The more active they become in the process, the easier it is to close the sale, or at least overcome objections that may arise. It is great to have both the husband and wife involved in the measurement process. Again, this is an opportunity to use your customers' name. During the process you might say, "Bill will you walk this end over to the wall for me?" Or, "Janet, would you mind writing down the measurements that Bill and I give you?" This is a process, an affair, a big deal. After all you are going to ask them to part with a significant amount of their hard earned dollars. Aren't you?

Asking questions during this process along with casual conversation seems to work best. An office or trophy room is a great place to get them to talk about themselves. Let's face it, besides hearing their own name they also like talking about themselves. Be careful here though. I was in a house one time and said "wow, that is an awesome swordfish, I love fishing". The response was not what I expected or hoped for. She said to me, "that jerk ex-husband of mine hasn't come to get that yet I would like to throw it in the trash. I wonder what he was really doing on those fishing trips". So be careful in taking an active interest in someone's hobby, it may not be their hobby. It may create some negative memories and make it difficult for them to listen to what you are saying. Whatever you do, make sure you don't lie about a sport or hobby. Your client will be sure to ask or talk about things a real _____ enthusiast knows about. If you blow your credibility during this portion of the presentation you might as well go home.

Make this a pleasurable event. Explain why a heat gain heat loss calculation is so important. Explain the negative effect of improperly sized equipment. Explain about placement of supplies and returns. Speak in terms like, "we will put the three way supply diffuser over her, so that the cool air blankets this hot wall. The return will go here so that we can obtain great humidity control and circulation in this room". You are keeping them involved and having them take ownership of the system and installation.

10

The equipment inspection

After the room by room measurement is complete you now want to take a look at the equipment. You say, "O.k. Bill and Janet, the measurement's are complete, could we take a look at the equipment now"? Again, using their name, and having them take some control. Many times this is the first place they want to take you, only because most of your competitors walk in the front door and say, "where's the furnace". So your customer is pre-conditioned to take you right downstairs to look at the furnace. Or they will say, "The furnace is over there", and they point towards the basement door. That is because others only asked for the customer to show them where the furnace is located, and the customer didn't even go with them.

This is a major reason why you explain the steps of YOUR process. Remember earlier I talked about the up-front verbal contract. If you explain to them the steps that are taken, and you ask their approval of the steps, there are no surprises. I have heard many variations of the up-front contract, and you have to incorporate what works best or is most comfortable to you. It has to be in your own words and in your own style. Everything you do in the process has to be natural and not seem like a written script. I personally do not use and can't stand page by page script books. Yes you need a book with letters, and a book showing actual installations, but a page by page "read along" is boring and unprofessional. Again, set up the steps you are going to take and explain them. After you explain them ask a question such as, "fair enough", "Does that sound fair to you". Or something to that nature. Once you have set that up make sure you follow the steps. Make it natural. Now, back to the equipment inspection/evaluation.

The inspection of the equipment is a great way to transition from a "salesperson" to a technician. Even though you are not a technician and never said you were, your actions transform you to a degree in their subconscious. You are primarily lowering their guard to make the process more comfortable. In fact all of these things you are doing are slowly chopping down the fence piece by piece. It is an ever so accurate piece by piece process but it works if you work it.

When you go down to the equipment, or wherever it is located, make sure you have your digital camera and flashlight. You will also want to make sure you have your "existing equipment evaluation form". This may be part of your structured needs analysis which we spoke about earlier. You will write down existing furnace make, model and btu/h information. In order to find this you may have to remove the front panel. I love this part. It serves two purposes. One, it gives you further credibility, and two, the panel is left off for later in case they ask to speak alone for a few minutes. Make sure you write down gas piping size, supply and return dimensions as well as electrical information. Go over to the panel and open up the electrical panel and write down if it is a 200 amp panel and count how many open spaces. You are most likely the only person who has done that. Take pictures of the equipment and the electrical panel.

Now that you are inspecting the equipment you want to make special note of the one inch filter. I love to take out that throw away filter and purposely have a difficult time putting it back in. Because I guarantee they have a hard time each and every time, and when you make the recommendation for the "easy to change" high efficiency filtration, the pain of the tough filter change will come to the forefront. You do not want to say much during this process, you want to make slight physical notations.

You may touch a rusty area of the furnace interior. You may touch an open part of the exposed duct. I like to make a little noise while touching it. Nothing terribly negative because you do not want to insult that fine inefficient equipment they have been feeding for twenty years. A point of your flashlight and an "hmmm" should suffice. Yes, this is used most often in the automobile dealership during the appraisal of your trade in. The used car manager is walking around and may touch or feel a dent or rust spot. This is simply lowering the value of the trade in your mind. Your sub-conscious mind no doubt. The sub-conscious is where we need to be in order to make the sale. You want to subconsciously be pointing out the negatives of the system.

If you notice a small oil leak near the oil filter or oil line you may want to say "has this been leaking a long time Bob?" Your reply is that we replace the oil line and filter as a standard. "We also make sure the oil line is copper and sleeved Bob, as that is Massachusetts Code". Again, chances are your competitors said nothing about any of this stuff. In all actuality you are discrediting them without saying anything directly negative about them, their product or their company. Let the customer come to their own conclusion. The 'aha" moments build up in their mind until the only logical solution based on emotion is to do business with YOU!

While you are in the equipment area you will also write down information on other mechanical items. Even though they haven't asked you for a price on a hot water heater or a humidifier, if it is beneficial to them and it needs replacing you can offer the replacement. Chances are if you don't offer it, you will never sell it. I also like to say, "Listen Bob and Janet, the reason I am taking the information off of this other equipment is because we keep a data base of your equipment. This way, should you have a problem with these in the future; we have all the information we need to provide fast accurate service for you". "Is that acceptable to you?" Another small commitment and trial closing question. You have their heads going up and down in the yes motion so many times and for so long, that it will be hard for them to change direction in the end. Asking their permission on these things goes a long way in building rapport and credibility. You are not a pushy salesperson; you are a polite, consultative professional looking to help them with their home comfort needs.

The basis of all these steps is to differentiate and build value. If you can effectively do this each and every time, you will sell more with a higher average sale amount. You will also have happier customers which refer more friends, relatives and co-workers to you.

11

The recommendations

The preso, the grand finale, the show, the game, the big finale…
"Call it what you like, if you can't close the rest doesn't matter".

This part is exactly where you're "Colombo" routine pays off. Your proper evaluation and investigation is used in fine detail during the final recommendations. You need to make sure that all the steps described previously were followed, and trust me, if you miss a step you'll know. I have missed steps many, many times and that is when the numbers go down, and your closing ratio falls short.

The difference between a true professional and a want to be is that the true professional recognizes this. The true professional looks at each presentation and determines what was good and what was bad. The pro does an analogy of each and every step to see how it could have been done better, and how to try something different next time. But a pro does not get negative and discouraged and change companies or jobs. A real sales professional does not blame others or blame the customers. If you start hearing yourself say things like, "why do I get all the bad leads". "These customers don't want to buy anything". Negative speech and negative thoughts will destroy your chances. Stay positive, always be learning and be persistent. Perseverance is very important in everything you do!

The time has come to discuss all the things you have learned throughout your investigation. You need to sit down in a place where the customer is comfortable, and a place where they normally conduct business. I find that the dining room table is a great place. On the other hand the family room or den is often too casual, but it really depends on the situation and your relationship with the client. I do know that you will need the full attention of both or all decision makers. This means that the kids need to be kept busy during this portion of the process. Getting the parents away from the children or vise versa can be difficult, especially after little Johnny helped with the measurement process and you have bonded with him as well. You become more of a real person when you pay some attention to the children. If little Johnny likes you the parents are more apt to like you as well.

If you find that the child or children may be disruptive during this portion it is time to play the coloring book game, or some similar approach. I like to bring a drawing of my truck along with some crayons. You can have the children play a little coloring game by coloring your truck. Of coarse they can easily see your clean well lettered truck out the front window because you parked strategically. This will keep the children busy, and build further trust within your customers mind. You may also want to add statements like, "my son Ryan loves to color my truck". Again, you are reinstating the fact that you are a father and a human being and not a mechanical script speaking sales person.

Now that you have their attention in a place you are all comfortable, you need to make sure of the seating arrangement.

You want to make sure that the parties are both in a position where you can make clear eye contact with both of them. In doing this it is probably likely that they will not be in a position to make eye contact with each other. This can surely throw a presentation off track, because one of the parties is thinking about what the other was trying to say through a gesture or eye movement. It may have been nothing, but you do not want to lose their attention on what you are saying.

You want to be natural and not nervous. To see a demonstration of this please watch my presentation at Comfortech Idol 2004. You can get a copy from Mr. Charlie Greer at Charlie@hvacprofitboosters.com

It was stated that many of the contestants showed signs of nervousness and had their ankles clenched. This can be perceived as dishonesty by some clients, and can be a quick killer to your potential sale. It takes a lot of practice and role playing to become smooth and natural during your presentation, but as soon as you master this you will start to see the results and have a lot of fun.

Your presentation starts out with a review of the needs analysis. You are going to highlight the areas of concern within the home. These are the things that they are looking to correct. Make sure your presentation and the equipment recommendations are directly in-line with their comfort concerns. Do not recommend equipment based solely because it is the quietest, or because it is very efficient. If these things are not important to them you are not building any value and your price whatever it may be, will be too high.

You need to make statements like, "Bill and Janet, you told me that cost of operation and dependability is important to you, is that correct?" "You also informed me that you were sick and tired of the uneven temperatures within the home, right?" "If I heard you correctly Bill, you stated a programmable thermostat would be something you would like to have?" Basically you are re-stating everything they told you. Essentially you are refreshing their memory on the reasons they would purchase a certain type of equipment.

Too many HVAC/R professionals sell or attempt to sell by model name. An HSXA19 means nothing to your customer. But a highly efficient super quiet outdoor unit that will provide ultimate humidity control and comfort does mean something to your client. You need to go line by line down your recommendation. Make sure they cannot see the price on the bottom of the page. The price needs to be on a separate page or you need to write it in after you go over all the equipment. Each piece of equipment is chosen because it has a certain benefit directly related to what they told you throughout your time together.

Continually re-affirm that the piece of equipment was chosen because it performs a certain value or task within the Home Comfort System. You might say,"this is the _____ high efficiency air filter. This will help filter out the pollen and airborne particulates that contribute to little Sally's allergies".

"Won't it be nice to provide some relief for those allergies?" You're already talking about them owning the system. Won't it? Not wouldn't it? Not only the words you choose but how you phrase them is very important in this part of the process. You are building value each and every time you ask a question like that. When the equipment you are recommending directly relates to their comfort concern and they see the relation that builds value.

You need to strategically go line by line explaining everything that will be done. Make reference to earlier conversations if possible. Such as, "this is the refrigerant line-set, that is the part I told you about that goes from the indoor unit to the outdoor unit". "You, know, the one that I explained we will cover with a piece that looks like your gutter". Do not assume they know what anything means, or that they know what any part is. A piece as simple as the "pad package" can leave them wondering. Make sure you explain what it is and what it does, why it's needed and how it relates to their specific needs or how it helps correct a certain problem they may have. Never over promise and under deliver. Never promise that it will cure Johnny's asthma. Simply state that it will **help** eliminate the particles that **may** contribute to Johnny's asthma.

When you get to the end of the equipment/installation specifications you need to ask them if you missed anything. Do not ask a question like "do you understand". Most customers will never admit that they don't understand, and they simply will not buy to make you understand that they don't understand what you were trying to sell them. Know that the reason they give you for not buying will be something different than what they told you. You may never find out the real reason they didn't buy.

As soon as you answered any initial questions they may have you need to move on. Your closing statement can be a million different things. I find it most effective to say something like "o.k. Bill and Janet, the system we just spoke about with the equipment we just discussed will be an investment of $22,897.00 THEN SHUT UP!!......

This is where most sales people lose it. You need to state the investment, because that is exactly what it is. It's an investment in their comfort, health, safety and piece of mind.

He who talks first loses. I like to write down the price as I am saying the numbers, while at the same time turning the price so they can clearly read it. Never say twenty two thousand dollars. (That sounds like a lot of money) Simply say, the investment will be 22,897 write it, turn the paper facing them and upside down for you and keep your mouth shut. If you have previously discussed payment or credit terms you can simply change your statement to "the monthly investment will be 246".

Wait for them to say something. No matter what they say make sure you repeat the objection in the form of a question. This takes some serious practice, but when you get good at it the fun begins. They say, "That price is too high" then I wait a second and say, "the price is too high?" In the form of a question. They will come back with a secondary objection, or they might say I could never afford that. Now you are on your way, you just need to find out how to make it affordable through one of your many finance programs. Price objection is the easiest objection to overcome.

That means you the company and the system are just fine, now you just need to help them find a way to pay for the system.

They may also sit in silence for a couple of minutes which may seem like an eternity. Just stay calm and composed and maintain eye contact with them. Do not start to fiddle with your pen or become uneasy. Be patient, you are asking them to spend a great deal of money!

If they come back with we would like to talk about this a little bit. Your answer will always agree in a way. You never want to become confrontational. Your answer will be, "great, my wife and I always discuss our investments together. Why don't I go start putting the furnace back together while you two talk". While you are saying this you are already getting out of your chair to go and put the furnace back together. This really doesn't allow any other option. What are they going to say "no, leave the furnace apart we would enjoy a night with no heat".

This is exactly why every step of the way is so important. That is why I stated leaving the furnace cover off during the equipment inspection is so important. You need to have an arsenal available and know how to use your arsenal. I love to ask the question, "besides price, is their anything else that we need to talk about?" "Is xyz heating the company you would like to do business with?" "Does the comfort system I am recommending meet all your home comfort needs?"

You need to really isolate the real reason or objection. Remember, people are conditioned from a very young age to put up a fight. Negotiation is taught and ingrained from a very young age. You negotiated with everyone from the minute you could communicate. You negotiated before you could even use words. Yes, I am sorry, the automobile business has also conditioned buyers to negotiate and put up a fight.

Once you really isolate the real and true reason they don't want to buy at that second, you can work on overcoming that objection. Never ever just drop price. I love to start taking things away, but you need to do this in a pleasant manner. I like to say things like, "hmm, if we don't install the humidifier now, we could save you _____ dollars". "But you did tell me Bob that Janet's dry skin really bothers her in the winter". "What part of the system do you think you could go without?" You have done such a great job at selling features and benefits there is no way they are going to want to do without anything.

One of my favorites is "if I could give you six months to come up with the money for this system Bob and Janet would that help?" The answer will mostly be "yes" "that would help". You then say, "I thought so". At that point you are reaching down to get the easy to fill out forms to give them the six months no payment no interest program. This is a form of the; if I could would you game that was made successful by the automobile business. You need to keep coming up with ways to help them, and more times than not one of the offerings in your bag will be exactly the special they are searching for. You are a comfort consultant and are there to help them find a way to make this happen.

Many sales professionals give up way too easy. The customer says no and they start packing up their stuff to leave. The word "no" is only telling you that they need clarification on something. Or they don't want to tell you they can't afford it. If during my home tour investigation I get the feeling money is tight I may use the four square closing game. This is the piece of paper with four different squares drawn on it, and in each different square there is a way to pay for the system. One square might say visa, master card, discover. The next might say $122 per month and the next might say $244 per month and the last might have the total investment number entered into the box. I will then say "o.k. circle the box that you like the most". Once that happens I go into the explanation of what that plan is, how it works and begin filling out a couple of forms.

I will say, "Yes, that is a very popular plan, I only need to ask you a couple of questions". You get the paperwork started and say, "please sign here Bob, and Janet I need your signature here". You take and keep control. This is s huge benefit of being organized and good at paperwork. Yes, I am great at this after spending many years in the dealership finance office. There is nobody better at getting through paperwork than the automobile dealership F&I (finance and insurance) manager. Better known as the F&I guy.

Make this whole process painless for your customer. Make it exciting and enjoyable. Once you have overcome the objections and finished the paperwork, put it away and talk about another subject. Do not go back to the deal, the equipment or anything about the sale unless they ask a question. Answer any questions directly and move on. Do not spend allot of time there after you are done. You do not want to be present if and when buyer's remorse sets in. Do your job and get on with it. Thank them for their business and let them know the next step. "Thank you very much Bob and Becky, I really appreciate your business. Bill

Smith our installation coordinator will be in touch to confirm the 27th installation".

Make sure you send a thank-you card. This thank you card needs to be sent even if you didn't close the sale at that time. I like to have the thank you card with me and I mail it as soon as I leave their house. I like to say to them, "Could you please tell me where the closest post office is; I need to mail something really important". Make sure the thank you has a hand written message and make sure you hand write the envelope. Use a stamp not metered mail. This is more personal. Sometimes if you mail this after an early morning appointment, they may just get the card the same day, or for sure they will get it the next day. This could be the difference of going with you or with someone else. Just another step at differentiating yourself from your competition.

If in fact you didn't close the sale, (you probably didn't follow the steps) make sure you have a mutually agreed upon next step. So many people walk out without establishing the next step in the process. In fact, the next step needs to be established regardless if you closed the sale or not. Make sure that whatever the agreed upon next step is you keep your end of the bargain. If they didn't buy during this appointment, make sure you know their projected decision time.

Most customers make the decision with forty-eight hours. It's your right to ask them when they were expecting to make up their minds. Make sure you ask if they have any additional questions before you leave. If it seems like they are right on the edge of the fence you can use the "schedule the installation" close. Basically that means that you call the office and speak to the installation manager and get their name on the installation schedule. This way they have the preferred installation date and time, and if something changes they can call and let you know. This is better than walking out with a hand shake and fido's saliva on your slacks.

No matter what you do, stay positive and do not get confrontational or put down the competition or the competitor's product. If you did your job properly they will be able to come to their own decision with the information you spoke about throughout the process. Many times the key to the close is in the success of you're after appointment contact. Follow up with a thank you and a call. E-mail if you have their e-mail address. Don't be bothersome; just simply ask if there are any questions they may have. Always thank them for their time and give them an easy way to contact you. At times the "please feel free to call me" line with your home phone number is a clincher. Be helpful, genuine and courteous.

If you follow these steps each and every time, I will guarantee you that your results will be significantly better than the results you are now achieving. You will have more fun, make more sales and as a result make more money. Can you live with those results?

Please let me know how you have employed these practices and the experiences you have had utilizing these tools. If you have any further questions, ideas or comments let me know. I am still learning every day, and striving to get better with each and every day. I think sales is the most enjoyable profession one can have, but if your not closing sales it is the most miserable job anyone can ever have. Make it a career and not a job!

12

Final thoughts

Regardless of what profession you are in the key to success in my opinion is having the will and determination to succeed. You need to constantly keep your mind open to new ideas and consistently remain in the learning mode. You can never have too much experience or education as it relates to your personal or professional growth. Markets, products and customers constantly change and if we are not changing with them we will be left behind.

The total success of yourself and your organization also depends upon the people on your team. The people on the "bus" need to share the same positive attitudes and need to be aligned with the same vision. The alignment of your "team" needs to be a vision that was set forth by everyone involved. People take greater ownership of a process when they have an integral part of the process development. You must make sure that you all have clear cut objectives along with standard operation procedures. These need to be developed as a team and tied into individual and team goals. These goals need to be posted and shared with everyone involved. Dates need to be set to review the progress towards these goals. Success in anything is a "we" not an "I" and no person is an island. Working together has tremendous results and benefits as long as your target goals are aligned and understood. The goals have to be realistic and if you are not getting there you need to look at them, determine the obstacle and the way to move forward. Readjustment of the goal is totally fine and is not failure.

I wish everyone the utmost in success and enjoyment in whatever you do. Success means different things to different people. Whatever your definition of success and happiness may be just go for it! You are the only one who can make the decision to do or be anything you can imagine. The inertia of forward moving success is absolutely unbelievable, and if you continue moving in that positive direction you have chosen, planned and mapped out, there will be nobody that will be able to stop you. It is nearly impossible to stop a moving locomotive. Believe me there will be many in your path that will tell you that you don't have what it takes, or that you will never do it. Don't worry, your positive attitude will force them to come along or move aside. There are only two things that accountability and focus can do to people. One, they can make the changes to accomplish the goal, or two, move aside and find a different place to spread the disease of negativism.

Believe it and you can achieve it!

About the Author

I grew up in the Northwest Suburbs of Chicago. During much of my younger life I worked with my father in the automobile dealership. I worked many positions within the dealership, and started with the position of washing cars. After a short time I moved to areas of the business which required use of my communication skills, which were evident at a very young age.

I spent many years in that business, and worked as a service advisor, new and used car salesperson, finance manager, sales manager and general sales manager. After many years in the Chicago area I moved with my wife whom is from Central Massachusetts, where we now reside with our two son's ages ten and twelve. I spent a few years as a licensed mortgage broker in Massachusetts, and eventually sold that business.

In 2002 I began my career in the HVAC/R industry working for a leading Massachusetts HVAC/R firm.

While employed by Mark E. Meacham, Inc. I began to see an area of expertise I truly enjoyed. This area is just now becoming popular throughout the United States, and I feel I am on the forefront of this industry known as IAQ.

Indoor air quality is a fast growing industry that encompasses many aspects of the air we breathe within our homes and businesses. Tremendous advancement is being made regarding the direct relation between asthma, allergies, headaches and lung irritation and the air we breathe at home and at work.

My knowledge and determination in this arena is allowing me to become the industry leader in IAQ and IAQ sales. I have successfully learned the HVAC/R industry and the IAQ industry while obtaining top-notch sales results. I have also helped many, many clients with indoor air and comfort.

Any individual interested in IAQ or sales in general must read this book. Anyone in sales that deals with the buying public can certainly benefit from this easy to read, easy to understand book about sales.

mjyoungs@charter.net
www.michaelyoungs.com

0-595-34960-9